Beyond Conscious Thought

Inspirational Messages
Volume I

Opening to Spirit Series

N. J. Fenttiman

Copyright © N.J. Fenttiman, 2020
Published: 2020 by
The Book Reality Experience

ISBN: 978-0-6489404-1-8 - Paperback 2nd Edition
ISBN: 978-0-6489404-9-4 - Ebook Edition

All rights reserved.

The right of N.J. Fenttiman to be identified as the author of this Work has been asserted by her in accordance with sections 77 and 78 of the Copyright, Designs and Patents Act 1988.

The information contained in this book is of a general nature and should not be regarded as legal advice or relied on for assistance in any particular circumstance or emergency situation.

The Publisher and author jointly or singularly, accept no responsibility or liability for any damage, loss or expense incurred as a result of the reliance on information contained in this book.

Any third party views or recommendations included in this book do not reflect the views of the Publisher, or indicate its commitment to a particular course of action.

No part of this publication may be reproduced, stored in a retrieval system, copied in any form or by any means, electronic, mechanical, photocopying, recording or otherwise transmitted without written permission from the publisher. You must not circulate this book in any format.

Cover design Luke Buxton | www.lukebuxton.com
From an original drawing by N.J. Fenttiman adapted by Lisa Townsend

To Patrick
The catalysis
'Always'

Introduction	i
The Committee	iii
Wisdom	1
Pearl	3
Power	5
Love	7
Innocence	9
The Cat	11
Joy	13
Colour	14
Trust	16
Opening To Spirit	18
Silence	20
Scattered	21
Communication	23
Peace	24
Fear Of The Unknown	26
The Rose	27
As A Tree	28
Questions	29
The Day	31
Intent	32

The Soft Rays Of Light	35
Why Fear Love?	37
The Rainbow	39
Patience	41
Company	43
Blueprint	45
Dust	46
Walk Softly	47
Words	48
My Garden	49
Again Patience	50
Joy Within	51
Step Into The Unknown	52
Reach Forth	54
Blessings	55
The Shadow	57
To Seek	59
Whispers	61
Sorrow	62
Joy Of Sharing	64
Promise	65
Vigilance	66

Distance	68
Inner Peace	69
Sincerity	71
Book Of Records	73
Listen	74
Actions	75
Everything Speaks	77
Why Analyse?	78
Service	80
Daily Life	82
Self-Care	83
Change	85
Take Hold Of Life	87
Confused	88
Imagine	90
Look	91
The Child	92
To Each	93
Aspect	95
Informal	96
A Grain Of Sand	98
Three	101

Pathway	103
The Journey	105
Harmony	108
Found	110
Confounded	111
Acknowledgement	113
Clouds	114
The Way Ahead	116
Choice	118
Perception	120
Light	123
Responsibility Of Pleasure	124
Rest	125
The Gift	126
This & That	127
Healing	128
Love Itself	131
Acknowledgements	133
About the Author	134

Introduction

In recent decades there has been a renewed, almost urgent interest in the search for meaning and guidance in one's life and in the lives of many others. The 'church' not seeming to satisfy this desire left many, myself included, with a sense or a need to find a knowing, an understanding and a connectedness that would fill the void and heal the spirit.

Hello! I am Norma. I had for many years known that there was 'more' about me than I could logically perceive. My Mother was an 'intuitive' and often sensed death or illness about a person. She, therefore, tried to shield me from developing my intuition.

It was in 1994 (aged 51), when I enrolled in a Bachelor of Arts degree in English Studies, that I discovered a number of my colleagues had intuitive/psychic abilities. There were two mediums and a healer in my class.

"Why aren't you working?" I was asked "Me, how?" And so with Gwen and Marg's guidance and meditation, the process began.

I began to write - "Let the words flow, without conscious control." Many a page went into the bin. Finally, I stepped aside and trusted. And in that trust, so much more of my life and experiences made sense.

I was writing, I thought, for myself. Some days asking

for assistance and guidance, with life's difficulties and others for the pure joy of being 'in company'.

The words flowed from me as if I were a vessel; it is an amazing experience, they fill the mind and the senses before they hit the page, and at times with such a sense of 'pure' love, that you just want to stay in the space, just a moment or two longer.

It is a most incredible and powerful experience - both for this vessel and I hope for you, the reader - and can result in a euphoric sense of being; combine this with pure humility and a sense of wholeness is created.

Thus, these inspirational messages, this guidance may result in a shift of energy; which may trigger a deep emotional response; it may clarify personal issues and create a sense of healing.

> *"Share the words with those who would listen. For in this too we learn."*
>
> **(NF 28/3/1998)**

In love and light – you and I, journey together.

N.J. Fenttiman

The Committee

When I had been writing for some time, and had begun to move past the self-doubt, I was able to accept that the message, the wisdom, was beyond my conscious thought. The words just seemed to flow free of my consciousness.

It was at this point, I posed the question – "Who are you?" In reply the impression I received was of a group of beings, each with a specialty area of wisdom. The group would commune in unison – as one voice. However, if a specific explanation, or further detail was required, then 'the specialist' would step forward.

> *"It is with joy we greet thee,*
> *and would commune with thee in unison.*
> *We are many and would pass to thee words of love and of joy."*
>
> **(NF 8/2/2001)**

Thus in the reading you may be, at times, aware of the various tones and voices that come forward. The hint of an Irish lilt; the rhythm of a drum or heart beat; the gentle tone of a wise teacher or indeed the feeling and sense, within your heart of the pure unconditional love of a higher being – perhaps your own Guardian Angel.

And so, I opened to all of the impressions of 'The Committee'.

> *"Is it not more joyful to stand in company?*
> *As we who stand with thee."*

(NF 3/11/1997)

In love and light, always.

Messages can and do filter into this dimension.
When someone opens a channel
the messages, thoughts and feelings bring
love, joy and knowing.

* *** **

Go forward on your path
In knowledge and
Security and with
Love to share.

* *** **

I am. "I am"
I am the way
I am the light
You and I are one.
The universe connects all thought
In addition, your thoughts call to us.

* *** **

I am, you are, they are
As one linked by light, by love, by thought
Know me, know thy self.

* *** **

Walk in the light
Walk in the love
Walk in the truth – of all things
And of all life.

Wisdom

Good morning my child – know that I am with you, know that we are with you – always. The journey is long and we shall take it together, you and I and many others. You have the power at hand. Look at the wisdom within all creation for your strength. You my child are safe; you are protected in my love – by many on this side.

Come sit, let us rest and listen to nature. She whispers to all who wish to hear. What do you hear?

I hear the crickets' morning song.

Yes, they are busy as is all nature with its prayer.

All living things in nature give thanks to the ONE.

To the ONE present in all.

As the sun passes across the sky

So is wisdom.

As the moon fills the night

So is wisdom.

As the birds fly

So is wisdom

As the smallest creature crawls

So is wisdom.

All things are one

All things are one.

We who pass this way must stop and look within that we might know all things – all things are within thy reach. Just put forth thy hand and know it will be filled. Do not fear the love that is there for all to know.

The time is near when all shall be clear to thee; it is within thee now, however, you fight it. Fear not, the fight draws to a close and the joy fills thee – you have felt it, you know it.

Wisdom is like the bird that soars ever high. Each must reach out to the wisdom – each must extend their vision. True wisdom is in all things. True wisdom is around thee, and thee and around all. Do not *discount* the wisdom within.

Today we begin a journey of great length. It will be a journey of joy. A journey of love. There is great promise as we step out together. Join us, as there are many messages for those who wish to hear. Many will question – their answers will come – fear not.

Pearl

Now let us begin with peace and calm – all noise ended. You have travelled far in the past few days. We are proud of you. Your patience and steadfast encouragement have shown proof of your ability to find a way through to a lost and confused soul. With your help, he opened the door. With your help, we got a foot in.

Now for today's pearl – which you collect and will thread with many others –

> Cleansing of all
> Cleansing of thee
> Take time and love.

We cleanse our body; we cleanse our mind and heart. Cleanse the spirit within and without, that we may open to His wisdom, His joy, and His love.

To cleanse oneself is to bathe away all fear, all earthly entanglements – wash thyself in the river of love.

To cleanse one's soul, open to the light and reach out with inner joy, reach out with inner knowing.

To cleanse the mind and heart, open both that you may know and feel with clarity all that is within thee.

In days of old, cleansing was by fire. Heat and smoke removed all traces of fear and darkness.

With the candle, you remove fear and darkness, but remember the candle within – it shines bright in thee.

Speak these words to others, that we may all join together with the One who lights all paths to truth and beauty.

You are going on a journey of light discovery. Cleanse thy feet and step forward. Cleanse thy heart and know thy way.

Remembering to brush the flowers as you pass – even unto the smallest.

Power

Today we shall work on Power, the power within – in us all to control others. It is a power we must moderate and temper with love.

Power is within all and when used *for* others it blossoms as love. Power is the seed of the life force. The strength with which to push ahead. To move forward. Power dominates the earth at present; this power is false and must be tempered. It must be balanced with wisdom and love for the good of all living beings.

Power shines as a star in the night and can lead those who will follow its light. Those who follow this light must, however, be discerning – they must question, they must understand. Do not follow blindly. Do not surrender individual power. Do not force your power upon another.

** *** ***

Now let us move ahead, just a little way – know we come from the light and would speak with thee about matters important to thee and to others nearby.

One must see – see what is before thee.
One must know – know what is before thee.
One must care – care for all who come to thee.
Give of thyself that others may grow.
All that you give will be replenished.
Know we support thee.

Love

Today we will speak of love – you find this word difficult to say at present yet you are filled with love for all living things.

LOVE

Love is all around
It is in the petal of the rose
And in the worms of the earth.

Love surges through all living things.
Love shines from the darkest corner
When least expected.
Love transcends life, as we know it.

True love, unconditional love
Cannot be denied
Cannot be destroyed.

Love can, however,
Be overlooked from time to time
But it finds its way to all
Even those in ignorance of its being.

> Love is. Love shines in all.
> And love is like a beacon
> Drawing us to its radiance.

** *** ***

Each of you who are filled with light – emit a radiance of joy and love, thus drawing others who would know and share this radiance. Do not fear this love.

Do not struggle with the word, as many need to hear it. They will understand the intent with which it is spoken. They in turn will know how to share this love, this circle of pure joy and the delight in living as one with the One.

All comes back to the One who is within and without. This radiance grows ever strong. Day by day new radiance pushes aside the darkness. Day by day, we open our hearts to light and love. As each day dawns, so does love. The cycle cannot be broken, it may be interrupted or even stalled but it cannot now be broken. The momentum gives it strength, many move with the strength. Take heart, take love, reach out and take flight.

Trust is Love.

Innocence

Good morning child, we are pleased to sit with you. We have much to do and much to share.

Now, let us speak of innocence, the childlike quality that fills all living beings. The quality most abused. The innocent child is often abused by others and we in turn abuse the innocent child within.

Innocence is not ignorance. It is beauty and pure unconditional love. A love of everything. An understanding of life. But as we grow we hide this innocence away. As we grow, we re-interrupt life.

Innocence when abused withdraws and hides. Beauty and love give way to fear and contempt. The innocent child grows to hate. To hate and mistrust oneself and those about them, and yet a spark of beauty and love lays hidden within and with true love may again blossom.

Those of you who retain the gift of innocence must acknowledge and share this gift with others. Look back to the innocence of childhood, the wonder, the joy, the anticipation of life itself. Immerse your being daily in this innocence. Renew each morning the pleasure of life. Look about and renew your wonder, your joy and let each day be filled with anticipation. The anticipation of knowing that this life holds for each and every one the key to understanding and wisdom – through innocence. We do not refer to naivety, you must each look about and be discerning. Be alert and aware of your situation and of those about you. Trust your instinct and your inner knowing to guide you.

Know each day brings joy through innocent vision and know each day presents pitfalls. Be aware but do not recoil from life's pitfalls. Those that trip you do so for your growth and development. You have choices, you may grow and blossom or you may cry and retreat. To those who wish to grow we offer help and guidance through love and innocence. Look about you, the help and guidance is at hand, it is in everything, we are in everything. No lesson is too small or too large for those who face the lesson.

It is only when fear dominates that the lesson becomes too great. Fear clouds the joy of innocence. Open your hearts and minds to the wonder of childlike innocence. Let the child within grow in love and beauty. Beauty of heart and mind and spirit.

Those who were abused in childhood have the spark of innocence deep within, stretch out your light and love that those who seek to open the heart may be guided. Each of you radiates an innocence that can be recognised. Those in need will know and understand the signs. They, when ready will reach out and take hold of the light you offer. Just reach out and radiate joy and love. Those in need will answer. You may never know whom you touch but they will know and they will share – so it goes around.

Innocence of mind and heart, blossoms and seeds in unknown fields far from our vision but the process has begun. Each blossom shares its seed in untold fields. You are the nurturers – spread the joy of innocence.

The Cat

Greetings – know that what we share, you must also share. The cat represents time through the ages. It carries the wisdom of the ages behind its eyes. Those that may read this wisdom must look deep into the eyes. Cats may cross your path or walk into your dreams – watch for the messages they carry.

*(A stray cat came into my life –
at a time when I needed company).*

This one is curious and likewise needs your company at present. He came to you as a gift but is not yours to keep. He also brings joy to others.

What do cats tell you about yourself? Are they not curious? Are they not still? Cats sleep long hours – they go within. Explore the darkness then come out into the light, and as the cat chose you – choose your own master. Find your own place of peace and tranquillity. Spend time grooming your spirit, knowing every minute aspect without and within. Utilise the 'nine' lives – some have passed but many lie ahead – use this one to regenerate and strengthen your resolve. Do not push ahead, relax and know the moment.

As the cat awakens from a long sleep, you are awakening but remember to be catlike – stretch and enjoy the sensation. Take time to groom, then sit and purr as you ponder your next move. The cat pounces only after clear, concise deliberation.

Be aware of the habits and mannerisms of the animals in your life. What can you learn from them?

Joy

Let us begin – today we will speak of joy. An emotion that is easily shared with others. Joy brings sunlight to even the hardest heart. It may sneak through the tiniest crack. Joy cannot be ignored.

However, where is it to be found? You may ask.

Joy is all about one. It is in the teardrop that greets new life and in the raindrop that creates new growth. It is a newborn kitten being cleaned by its mother. The smell of rain, the glow of the sunflower. Joy is in a stranger's smile. Joy is all around but some choose to ignore its presence.

Your world would be happier and safer with a little more joy. One cannot argue and fight if they have the giggles or if they are filled with and surrounded by pure joy. The joy of the moment, the joy of being.

All living beings experience joy. The monkey grooming its mate – the joy of finding a flea. The joy of eating that same flea. Watch the monkeys. Watch nature as it enjoys each day.

Simplicity of thought and word and silence. The silence is where you find us, as now. Set time aside each day that is convenient, that we may grow together.

You are an anchor, a peaceful and tranquil bay.

Colour

My child, colour is a living essence. It is in everything and it is everywhere. Even the blackness contains colour. All of the colours visible in the light, are contained in the darkness. They are just temporarily obscured from our vision, from our thought centre and sometimes from our belief. In this latter state, we allow in fear where there is no fear, where there is no need of fear. Do not cultivate this essence of life for it drains life and colour from one's daily living.

Colour enriches and enlivens all it encompasses. Let colour guide one – to health, to beauty and to nature, where it is so prolific. Observe the colours that share your day, those that stand forward and draw attention. What does that colour signify? Why has it drawn your attention? Is it asking you to take note of some specific event, occasion or happening that may be occurring in your life at present? Or perhaps it is guiding you to new horizons in life? Perhaps it warns of a lack of energy and vitality – note your health.

Each colour has a specific purpose as all indigenous peoples know. As do animals. Colours of warning, of temptation, of sharing and giving – fruits of the earth. Look about at colours and note their neighbours in true natural surroundings. Note the creatures that visit and frequent certain colours. We do not always see the plant's response to its visitors, but occasionally in your nature programs, you are granted a glimpse of nature's response – and there is always a response, just as you respond to colour.

Some colours make you feel good, energetic and inquisitive. Others create a sombre atmosphere, or an atmosphere of rest and tranquillity. Others awaken hidden fears in some, but colour itself does not create this fear. Colour is a neutral essence that attracts some and repels others.

Colour works on the sense of sight and may be observed to change with the hour of the day. Colour is associated with earliest recollections of childhood memories and adventures. Just as a sound or a smell recalls memory, so too does colour. Every part of the living being is connected to and with colour. Draw colour to your life, to your day, by acknowledging your awareness of colour. It is in your garden, your home and in your very skin, hair and eyes.

Colour radiates out from every living being. It sends its energy forth to mingle with other energies. Many see these waves of energy as they pulse out into the universe, as signals of being. Of being one with all. We are all interconnected and the colour vibration is but one way of connecting with and communicating with others of like-minded vibrations. As your colours pulse, so they connect with or brush by many. Some feel the wave of energy, others see it.

Colour is important in life, it is a necessary vibration bringing colour to the lives of others. Many search too widely, when all they need is an introduction to colour – it opens many doors for those who truly search and desire to grow and share.

Go in love, go in colour

Trust

Trust is like a leap – a leap of faith. Are you prepared to take this leap into the unknown? *I am nervous, but, I will trust.*

Good, now we begin – for today we speak of this trust, this faith. In the unknown, the unseen and in the void created by man that overwhelms faith, faith may diminish. Faith is not something that can be seen or felt. It is not tangible, it places every fibre of your being on alert. Danger! Unknown! Fear!

However, when you link with the energies about you, the natural positive energies and with the all-knowing high One, and when you trust your own higher self; faith, belief, trust and clear understanding follows.

The instinct is powerful, it is this instinct that guards and protects all of those whom trust – trust and instinct are the two sides of one, and we are one with all. Trust and faith are reached early by some, later by others and some never reach this state of being. If they do not trust and have faith in their own ability in their own being, they will never reach this outer state of peace. If it is not within, it cannot be without. They close, shrink with fear and they become aggressive and angry. They seek power, dominance over those whom they see as meek and soft. But these unbelievers underestimate the meek, the faithful. This is not a 'religious' faithful; more those who are filled with faith and who believe in themselves and in those about them.

Do not fear when your faith wavers for in these moments your faith is strengthened. Each trial, each tribulation, strengthens the believer's faith – to doubt is human but to dwell on the doubts is to retreat. A moment's hesitation is natural but always move ahead – note the trials and strengthen your resolve. Remembering always that we are one with all.

Go now in trust and knowing.

Opening To Spirit

What shall we speak of today child?

Opening to Spirit.

In opening to spirit, we must realise that a channel or higher connection has been made. A link to our own higher energy and thus to other energy and thus to other energies within this dimension. You create an opening, a link with a near dimension.

A dimension of sound and energy and of vibration and light, where thought is the connecting link to and for all beings. We can move from this dimension to yours via thought waves, just as you can link with us by thought patterns. Doubt is natural as there is much you do not yet understand. You doubt these thoughts. Persist.

Now a thought moves through space in an instant and it is always acknowledged or as you might say – received, even if you doubt that there is anyone listening. We always listen. But many of you direct your thoughts outwardly, when you should in fact direct many inwards. Many are afraid to look inward, but do you not know yourself? Why are you afraid of the now? The past can no longer harm one. To enjoy the now, and to prepare for the future, one must look inward, not to dwell in the past but to acknowledge it and to let it go.

If the past is hindering the now, it must be addressed but in the correct perspective of its happening. Do not drag it into the now, but look at the NOW event or situation that has required the recall of the past. Look inwards, to address the now, and get on with living.

Be childlike – laugh and cry, dance and sing, bring the youth and love forward into the now to open the window of joy in the future.

Giving and receiving go both ways, give that you may receive and receive that you may give.

The now is a time of regenerating and setting down roots. Roots that hold you firm for the present, bringing your energies back into balance.

Silence

Good morning dear friends. Please show me how I can maintain an opening for spirit.

Silence is the key but trust and love are essential. Each new step you take brings you to your goals, and to the goals of the universe of which you are a part. Your patience is rewarded and your knowledge and love grows daily. Your desire to share is being rewarded. By duty, care and example you share your spirit essence.

Go, be silent and open the heart.

Scattered

Good morning child. Today we sit with thee in peace and harmony. Your thoughts are scattered to the four winds at present but calm will prevail, do not fret. Harmonise the strings of your life and release a sweet song. This song is locked within but it vibrates and awakens the joy of release as you open to the One of joy and love. Your song will be heard and shared by many. Some near to you will rejoice in the song and they too will resonate and share with others in joy and love.

The peace you seek is within. Do not allow trivial life expectancies and disappointments to throw you off course. This is life – learn to go with the flow. You cannot guide and govern daily interruptions but you can accept them. Each problem will eventually dissipate and be resolved satisfactorily.

Harmony and peace resonate to all who seek them. And the rewards are great. Seek harmony in all life. Observe life in its natural form and delight in its harmony. It is found in sound and in movement. Watch the birds and animals and listen to their voices. They harmonise even when alert. Feel the call of nature deep within your being as you are all connected. Man has misplaced this natural sensation; look for it, feel it, know it – harmonise with life.

Peace is all around, in the sunbeam and in the clouds

you watch – it is the depth of knowing, the silence of living, the moment of birth and the moment of death, as this moment creates new life. Peace is the touch of love, the joy of sharing. It is in a moment, it is in a lifetime. Peace is akin to unconditional love – one without the other would create imbalance. Where there is true peace of mind and heart – there is love. True love.

Take charge of every moment and fill the moments with peace and harmony – you share these with others, why not allow them into your own life? Take care, take charge, take love into yourself, and then share with others. We cannot share that which we do not have.

Go in love.

Communication

Good morning, child, we are here. Communication can be difficult, the link must be established then held firm – it grows stronger, be patient.

Communication links all, you need only to be aware of this energy, this power. So much can be achieved, so much shall be achieved by clear and concise communication. Many communicate falsely and in selfish ways; there is much damage in such falsehoods. Keep your communication with others clear and concise. You have no need of falsehood. Open your heart and mind a little more each day, and note the communication that links with you. Note all levels and be aware of the messages that come your way – as in your dreams.

Peace

Today we shall speak of peace, the peace and silence that escapes many. The silence and peace is always there, you have but to sit and let the earthly distractions fall away.

An easy exercise is to fill the mouth and head with air – hold it for as long as possible – concentrate on the feeling – then expel it with force, two or three times then relax into your breathing. Call your guides in with this prayer:

> Spiritual friends and guides
> I call upon your help and protection
> During this meditation.
> I ask your help in opening to the
> Wisdom of old.

Sitting is not just a habit, it is a ritual. Meditation is a connecting and must be taken in sincerity. There are many types of meditation and each should be approached sincerely if the goal is to be achieved. To relax one must desire true peace and relaxation and must meditate in true sincerity.

** *** **

There is time for all in this world to do as they wish, if only they take hold of each precious moment. The exploited find joy in small moments and could give example to many. Hardship does not go unrecorded – infliction is most definitely recorded.

Beware those who perpetrate.

Find a quiet place – open the heart chakra, let it flow free of restraint, let it whirl.

Fear Of The Unknown

Good morning. To begin, look about this world at the present chaos; there is unrest in so many places. Many fear the unrest but if they would look deeper, it is within. All movement causes unrest but we cannot advance without movement.

Chaos is created when movement is required but we resist the call, the surge of energy. Many do not acknowledge this energy, do not heed the need for movement – whether it be physical or spiritual. So chaos is created by the fear of the unknown, and fear feeds on chaos. So it grows. Fear breeds hatred and suspicion and so man turns against his brother.

This fear must be overcome and light is the answer. A new balance of light and dark must be found, drawing the scale into balance once again. Those who know must fill each moment with light and share that light with others, sending it forth to balance the fear. To quell fear it must be checked, for it runs wild at present in this world but its run is now limited and it knows its free reign is ending – the light will prevail.

Go in light, and share.

If I can see but one star in the dark sky,
then I know that I am loved.

The Rose

Good morning dear child. Are there not roses in your garden? *Yes.* Each rose, each petal represents new life, beauty and contentment. Do they not flower regularly unattended? *Yes.*

They strive and grow and they share their life with whoever passes – if they were to but look sideways as they pass.

Occasionally, child look sideways at the life and beauty about you. Especially if it grows wild and unattended, it is still reaching forth to share its day with others.

As A Tree

Hello, child, we come when you call, but know that we are about you at all times. It is, is it not, a time for joy and love when we sit with thee?

Yes, dear friends, it is.

Now child let us work, you worry about so many and this is to your merit, but know that they can take care of themselves. We are proud of you, of your efforts, there are many here who send best wishes. Know that you are loved and that you are not alone, even now the space there is filled – do you not feel the energy about you? *Yes, there is comfort in the room, thank you.* You are welcome, I'm sure. We are here, just a whisper away.

You have come far and you do learn well, the fruits will be many, as the tree develops. You are as a tree, the roots are now well down and firm. The trunk is steady and straight and the limbs branch out steadfast and strong. The blooms are set – now you must await the fruit. The fruit is of your labour and shall reward you.

Questions

Yes, child, we sit and we are always with thee. What is it you wish – should we just sit or are there questions?

There are so many questions but I feel I intrude or ask too much.

There is no intrusion as we are all of one mind and share in this life. Questions are to be answered but only if they are asked. Did your mother not teach you, 'Ask and thou shalt receive.' Abide by this principle.

It just seems selfish to take up your precious time.

Our time is not like yours and there is nothing so precious as time well spent. We are here to be of service. Why not use the service that is offered?

Would you share a little pearl of wisdom with me?

Let the pearls fall upon the ground and be absorbed into the earth as tears of joy and love. As such, there is no waste. From the pearls, spring forth much abundance and when this abundance is scattered forth all may share; for if the pearls had been gathered up, only the one would profit.

Do you see how you may help others? Spread your pearls upon the ground afore you, that others may gather what they need. Ask only that they share their light and love with others. In this sharing, many will profit.

** *** **

We are always by – just reach out and we shall touch. Call and we shall answer. There is much that puzzles you and others but all shall be revealed in time and in the right order. There is an order of things small and vast, but to each the time will come nigh.

Do not fret, all is well.

Come now the day grows and there is much to do – you are filled with peace and harmony, go with us as one in love and light. Throughout this time, we are as one.

We go now, but only as far as your call may reach. Love and light always be yours.

Thank you.

The Day

Good morning, child, we greet you and welcome this opportunity.

There is so much to do and so much to learn. Yes, you have come far and know that the road ahead is still quite far. There is time to do all that is necessary, all that is required and all that is agreed. We walk together as have we always. The earth time weighs on you but in growth and love, you bloom forth.

Proceed with the day ahead and look to one day at a time. Achievements come by small portions. We sometimes do not recognise the achievements, because we overlook these small portions. There is often a very large message in a small object or word – *be alert*. The big achievements can be seen and known by all, but it is the small ones that may be of great importance to the individual. These are the ones that boost you and carry you ever forward.

Intent

Good morning, dear one – yes we are with you. There is much ahead in this day and all will be achieved. You doubt too much your own efforts. Do not, as you can achieve all that you intend. All that is needed and desired is the clear intent.

Just make a start and all will go well with thee. It is the first step on each venture that is the hardest, but once taken the following steps become easier. You know within that you can do this task.

Now shall we mull over a thought or two? What do you think of time? *It is used as a measure and it seems to restrict life.*

Yes, too much emphasis is placed upon 'time' but it can be freed to work with you and for you. Work by the body clock as best and as often as you can, and trust the instinct you naturally have for time. In this way far more can be achieved.

Have you not found that an hour or two of sleep may seem much longer, and when you only have one hour to achieve something, it seems like three and the task is completed well and early? *Yes, I have found this to be so.*

Another area of thought to be mused upon, is the domain of patience. Is this not a whimsical domain? Patience is not an aspect of life to be resisted or struggle against. It is to be an exercise of give and flow. Flow with, not against, and you and others need not struggle.

Patience is like time – you need to go with the body's instinct and know, as your inner one knows, that patience is a time of rest. The body recoups in this period of waiting – let it take its rest and do not fight these periods of 'patience'. You will grow and gather from these spells of patience.

You have much to do and we will assist. Go forth in love and light, the knowledge is within – open just a little and it will flow.

Thank You

Dear friends – thank you seems to be such a small offering, but it is given in sincere intent.

It is taken, as it is well meant, but it is the offering that is recognised, no matter the size. It is truly the intent that is noticed and recorded.

The Soft Rays Of Light

Is it not a beautiful morning with soft rays of light? Do you wonder at the power and love that the softness enfolds?

The mighty may be soft and gentle, and they may be mistaken for fools. But it is those foolish ones who look only for power who fall foul of ignorance. They write ignorance into 'their' belief, as they look only to power and see not the inherent power of gentleness.

Some see gentleness and softness as weakness, but does not a truly powerful being balance power with understanding, tolerance and humility?

Enjoy the soft glow of the dawn for it holds the power of light and life.

Be tolerant, understanding and gentle in your dealings, and in this others will see and know your power. We do not need to hit others about the ears for them to see and to know. Observance of others teaches us much. We may learn right and wrong, and in each, we have choice. We must each choose our path, but some see only the path of self, of self desire, of self power and of self wealth. But what are these if they are held in and smothered? If they are smothered and held only to one, they are trapped and cannot 'mother'. Open forth the arms and let this wealth and power flow out to all – that healing and growth may continue to circle all.

Do not break the chain. Greed, selfish acts and fear break the link of life and affects all around, all who are in the vicinity and these effects ripple outward touching many. We must counter these ripples with the soft rays of light.

A voice in the wilderness is a soft ray of light trying to penetrate the gloom, and even one voice holds true power. Never forget the power of an individual thought – good or bad.

Go now in love and light – to send out your rays.

Why Fear Love?

Greetings, we stand about you and offer love. When we take up the love, for it should be taken up, we become part of the One with all. Part of the chain of light and love, that links with life and living. Those who do not take up the love wither and fall into darkness. To hold the chain together those with love need to share. As it is given so to, you give – even unto those who do not see and to those who would ignore.

Many are afraid of love; it may be seen as a trap or as a weapon. Respect this fear but nurture those souls, remembering that the love they may have experienced perhaps had been bound with conditional ribbons. Conditions that they could not truly honour. Offer love that is free, love that does not require return, love that may flow to them and around them, and leaving a little that it may flow on freely to others. This love grows in strength and beauty, it frees the soul. This love, in its pure unconditional state cannot strangle and stifle one. This love shatters the darkest corner of fear. This love sets the soul afire.

Encourage the fearful to pick up the burden of love and delight in their realization of joy, not fear. We are here to help, but even we need help to encourage some.

The sum in the total is in gathering in the few, but gather

them gently and slowly, as fear dispels gradually and grudgingly. Fear not the fear, for love shines about thee, and child you need only radiate this gift.

Is not the voice of the bell clear and beautiful in its radiated sound? Do you not *feel* and *hear* its resonance? There is love in the vibration of the *toll*. Send on this love to all others. Let them feel and hear the vibration of our love.

> *Go now in peace and love and*
> *feel these throughout your day.*
> *Amen*

The Rainbow

Good morning dear friends.

We are always here, you do not need to call, but call you may and as often as you wish – dear child.

What of the Rainbow? Is it not a bridge that spans all and does it not bring joy and delight to all who gaze upon it. This is yet another vibration that may be seen and shared by many.

The rainbow bridges a great distance in a mere moment and shares its glory with all who look to it. Is it not strange that some see but *do not* see? They look only with the eye and not with the heart. To appreciate the true beauty of the rainbow one must look not only with the eye but with the *whole* being inner and outer, and they must be as one, to *truly see* all. Just as the rainbow is balanced across the sky, so too we must find and maintain that balance. It is not easy, as the rainbow is made up of droplets – a mere droplet may alter our balance.

Be ever vigil in thy efforts and know that a slight tilt in the scale of balance is not fatal, it is nature and natural – all one needs at those times is a little correction and the balance shall swing back. Remember when loading the scale to load evenly and fairly. Remember this, whether it be your own or another's. Judge truly thy action, to self and those to others about thee. Do not load more than you can carry. For it is not necessary to carry all at one time. Balance the rainbow of life and enjoy and know the beauty of life.

We each have a place within this beauty and it is for the benefit of all – not just the few. How may we share this beauty? How may we have this beauty? Some may ask.

There are those who may need help, for they seek what is before them. They look to far ahead and do not see the gift at their very feet. They do not see the rainbow.

With love, these may be brought to true vision and in that vision they shall see.

Amen

Patience

Good morning, child, we are here with thee. Do you not sense the presence? Do you not sense the energy? The warmth of the outer sun warms the inner being. Feel the energy of life. Know that there is always something new occurring in life.

Nothing stands still, movement and growth fill every moment. There is an urgency in life but it is contained within a peaceful patience. Do not rush headlong at life, you all have time to step back and view the pathway. Take time to choose and know that choice is not set fast in concrete, it may be altered, amended or even re-chosen. Then again, you may remain with the first choice. Isn't life wonderful? Is it not filled with excitement and anticipation?

Life is fearful when excitement and anticipation diminish in strength and resolve. Some must again find a way to nurture life and to trust in and nurture the self. Take for instance those who despair, they allow this sensation to take hold, almost wallowing in the feeling and in the self-pity. How can you help these people? One may ask. Always and only by thy example, by thy trust, thy love and thy faith that lingers for all to embrace.

Look again to the sun and the rays that touch all, regardless of time or place. Even when out of sight we know the sun is in the sky. We trust in its light, we have faith in its being and it is in this light that all may be repaired and restored. Light is a constant. Light is. Draw back the shades and let the light in.

Gradually, despair will fade, just as the darkness fades ahead of the dawn.

*** *** ***

Do you smell the roses? Does anyone smell the roses? Time must be set aside to enjoy life's pleasures, just as we work so must we rest. Some fill their life with work, for they fear the time to rest. They lack the skill of play, of laughter and of love. They do not love the self. Learn these skills, practise them and share *life* with others. The best way to recall these skills, for they are skills, is to return within to the child – the child held these skills in tune with nature. The child knew the joy, the excitement and the anticipation of living – *Remember*!! Once again, be childlike and destroy the despair.

Open your petals and let in the rays of light, that they may nurture the future seeds of life. Then in time spread these seeds on fallow ground. Then rest and watch life sprout forth. Is it not a pleasure, to see new shoots pushing up from within the earth. Push forth new shoots that others may take pleasure in your growth. We do grow daily and it is good that others may delight and grow by stealth. Good example is the best cure.

Go, laugh and be joyful.

Company

Good morning, we stand before you and would speak.

I am content to know that I have company.

Remember child there is strength and safety within company and as a group much may be achieved. It is not necessary that one may step before another. But also remember that the individual is just that – an individual who has a voice within the company. Do not negate thy power. Do not hand it to others.

There is a time when the individual may step forward. But at such times, they must not lose sight of the company and the support that brings them to this place and time. Give credit – give dues.

Many, when they find success, forget or deny the love and support that has elevated them. The air becomes thin and they hold it only unto themselves. They see their success, their elevation, as a solo journey. Fools, they fool only themselves and in the process, they do end, by standing alone. But is it not more joyful to stand in company – as we who stand with thee?

Your word and our word is one, your thought and our thought is one – do not deny the thoughts that present in the mind. In saving the small spider (by putting the tiny creature on a violet leaf), you granted a gift of life. The spider fell from your glasses to remind you of the ebb of life – it may trap and enfold but it also represents life and its many and varied parts or segments.

Each segment, intricately woven, captures the vibration of movement. This pulses to the centre and then outward along each strand. All who may have a hold of the thread, will feel and know the meaning of the vibration, however slight.

Do not fear to take a hold of the web of life, for it has much to share with those who venture forth into the unknown. But, in turn, send this message back to the centre, that it may also radiate forth to others. Although the web holds opportunity it does not mean that you approach unguarded, for there are some who sit and draw in those who would hand over their life willingly to another, these who shy from responsibility and account.

Ever question and be alert, then take that which you know to be truth and radiate it forth. It is good to sit in true company, so much may be shared. We may share in the true presence of others and they in ours.

Is it not a beautiful day to work? Go in peace.

Blueprint

Greetings - there is much embedded in your blueprint and it now begins to surface. Many about you also awaken to hidden knowledge and you are party to this 'time' in nature.

Remember there is a reason in all, although at times we are blind to that reason. It is such times as these that our faith and trust must be staunch. They will be needed to hold the balance. There is nothing to fear as all has been agreed and the choice factor is ever present. Thoughts and feelings may be changed and in the change so too events are altered. Outcomes are altered.

Focus on the white dove and know its grace and beauty, the movement of the wing, the strength, the purpose. There is purpose in every movement. Learn to see the purpose in all, remembering nature is a good teacher.

Dust

We are with you child, always. Even as you watch the tiny specks of dust in the morning ray of sunlight. Each catches the light and floats about, gliding on the warmth of the ray. Are they not like eagles gliding on the thermals? Rainbows, webs and dust all share the beauty of the morning with you.

In each tiny rainbow *(from the crystal)* that dart about your room are the colours of the universe. All life is filled with rainbows. They fill our being and we radiate the colour to those who would take note. We can learn so much from these colours and from their radiance. They may be seen, they may be felt, or they may be known. But in one way or another, they can be noted.

Colour may also be used to help others in so many ways. It may be used in healing to smooth and placate the soul, to invigorate and uplift the mind and to enhance the body. There is colour in all that is and those who do not see colour may sense its presence.

When you feel the rhythm and beat of music imagine the colours that flow in that energy – feel the colours. As you sense an aura so you sense its colour, open to these sensations and the colours will open to you.

Go in peace.

Walk Softly

Hello, child, we come forward to speak with thee. In this quiet time, we may commune. I am of the One, the one in all that we are of. The one that touches all in life and spirit. The all, the one, the holiest of holy. You are of the One, as is each and every one. Walk softly in the presence and blunder not.

We are many, we are one. You are many, you are one. Walk gently, walk softly.

> Blue is the night, blue is the day
> Blue come hither from far away
> Blue is my lady fair and bright
> Blue is the lady of the light.

> Tempt her not,
> for blue has the power to unite.
> Unite in life,
> unite in love all that come forth.

It does not make sense.

Sense! Why must there be sense?

Words

Good morning, child, we are one and would sit with thee. Memories remind us of good and evil in the past. They remind us to achieve the best but we must not live in the memories, only glance back when necessary and bring forward only what is needed from the past event. Sadly, many look but do not find the lesson.

Go forth in light throughout the day, remembering to shed a little light where you may.

You search too hard – let the words come of their own accord. Words that flow easily contain much, you question the words but there is a deeper meaning not yet clear. Trust the words, for the word is One. From the word comes ALL meaning. This to one, that to another, those who read may make of their own meaning.

If we question as we write, we break the flow, but we do not say questions are wrong, just put them in the right place.

Learn to listen, for each may have a turn to speak. Then all shall be clear. There is much for you to do now, so go in peace.

Don't go!

We only step back a little.

My Garden

Dear child, we speak to you in every breath of wind, in the movement of the flowers and in the chorus of crickets. Is there not life and movement all about? An abundance of life in this small space?

Again Patience

Good morning, child, we are with you. There is much change in the air and a time of movement is heralded. The feeling of being all at sea will soon pass, it is just the ebb and flow of life. All will be clear in due course and the decisions, when made, will be the right decisions. But for now, you may rest and restore your energies. You will find the energy and the way when all is in place. It is a little like shuffling the cards, a good deal relies on a well shuffled deck – let the shuffling take place in care, as it is not time now to be rushing. Patience. Remember so much is achieved during periods of patience. Enjoy this time and let your growth spread sideways a little, not all growth is forward moving. Growth often occurs when unexpected and always after a period of rest.

Do you not love the rain? There will be new growth, it is triggered by the rain. Watch and learn. Each wisp of nature holds a lesson. If we wish to find it, it is there. We come again to patience and with it to a new growth in life and in wisdom. Hold forth thy arms to receive thy gifts, for there are many and these are for you.

Go about the daily chores – and be of good company.

Joy Within

Good morning, my dear child, we are with you now and always, just as we are with all and in all. For are we not all of the one? Is it not a beautiful day?

Yes it is.

> Circles within circles
> Time within time
> Life within life

All that we are and would be, is within. But it is that, that most never find, never experience; the peace and joy that is within. We search always in the without for that which we most need, never realising that need requires no search. Our true needs are all within.

We rely so much on the external world and on others, but true power, joy and love comes from within and should be shared freely without resistance or greed, and without measure. Remember always we are of the One and what we do to others, we do also to ourselves. To measure is to restrict the very essence of life. There are too few who do not measure their deeds, too few who give freely of their love and time. There are too few who are truly balanced within.

Amen

Step Into The Unknown

Good morning, child - child of wisdom, open thy mind and thy heart to receive all that is necessary for thy continuing journey. Is not the way clear now to proceed? And proceed you shall. We come to teach, would you listen?

Yes.

There are steps to follow, for each journey begins with a step. Often it is a step into the unknown, but with your permission, we may light the way. Remember there are lessons even in the smallest objects. A lesson need not be so big as to be noticed by all. When you see a symbol (such as the frog in the garden yesterday) look for its meaning – in that way we work together. Sometimes the message may seem harsh but in all we are nearby. Let life flow.

'New Dawn' stands forward to teach and to guide – in a gentle process of knowing and believing. Believing in what you know and trusting, in the new growth.

'New Dawn' will teach you to look into the heart of a flower and know its ways. Then you may reproduce it for others to see and to know.

'New Dawn' works with the hands and the heart, as 'Teacher' works with the mind and the heart – team work, do you not agree?

** *** **

All of what we need to do is in preparation – we need not rush at this time. This time is for family and friends, a time of joy and love, of sharing and of being. Being as one, with one. But the plans are laid before thee and the preparations done. Now we wait a little. Is it not exciting?

Do what is necessary for now, remembering the plan is before you and what is – is! Adjustments may be made on both sides, but if you choose your place and set your path, as you have long ago, then only that which is, may befall you. That which is not can do no harm. Put up your head and move on in light and love for this is thy path. It is the path you have chosen and walk along. The fall, the grazed knees are but small pit falls by the way and they remind you to take your rest, for all must rest, even we. Did you not learn that on the seventh day ---?

Take your lessons from nature, as the seed rests and then throws forth new life and energy so too do you. It is the seeds of nature that you must look to, and the sands of time reveal all. Does not each grain have its place in the scheme of things?

Go now about the day's business in light and love.

Thank you.

Reach Forth

Dear child, we are here, we gather, as the gentle breeze gathers in the leaves, so we gather together.

Does friendship not abound at this time? All is being smoothed ahead for those who seek the way, and there are many seekers, some known, some unknown, but they are about. Much happens now to enlighten those who observe. There is much to share and much to be shared. Dip your hand into the pot and draw out what is required for thy needs. The pot is deep and serves those who reach forth.

Bring forth the trumpet and sound it loud, for there are many who await the call. They will come. The time of action draws nigh. Fear not, for there are many kinds of action – is not writing an action? *Yes*. Do not jump ahead of the horse. Gentle one, your action is love and understanding and the sharing of these with those about you. Each is equipped for their task ahead – know this. You are well equipped, as are those you gather with. Each has the right equipment and knowledge for the tasks they choose and the time to choose is nigh.

Sway with the breeze, allow it to guide your flight. Trust that it will set you down on the right spot. Trust also that the time is right. We are here and would guide with love – trust thy knowing.

Blessings

Good morning dear friends.

Good morning, child, all goes well with thee?

Thank you, yes.

Shades of power, shades of energy – do not live in the shade, as all is within. Draw on the energy from within. Each and every one may be what they *will*. Will only that which is good for all, and do no other *harm*.

They gather, many come forth at this time and it is good. It is come. It raises up its hands on high and blesses all. All are blessed, not just a few.

This time is significant for so many, not just in the season, but in so many other ways as well. All will be made known, all shall be revealed to those who would hear. Know that we hear in many ways. It is not just those of this plain. They gather, as on many such plains of wisdom. Time is the essence of the One, they gather.

Do not fear for that which is, is. All is well with thee and with those about thee. You each grow in wisdom and light, and this is spread wide about each of thee. You draw in many to the fold. Those you love and those not yet met. We trawl as one, and many are the instruments. Do we not orchestrate in light and love? For only in this way all will be righted.

Do not ask questions only from the mind. Open the heart and let the question flow forth. We know, but you must ask, each must ask and even if the question is not yet quite clear, we read the intent.

Thank you.

The Shadow

Good morning, child – we sit, we gather, we encompass all. Is it not so? Everything and everyone has its place in the scheme of things, is this not said? So too it is. Listen awhile as we gather. We greet the sun, we greet the day, and we greet you.

Who are you?

I am the shadow that walks with thee. Where you go I go also. We walk as one. In thought and deed, we are one. We have good counsel.

Now let us share counsel with those who sit here. Go in and draw from the depths, that which is within. In that it may be placed forth upon the page for all to see and know.

Strike forth and bare the way ahead. Many will tread the path and it must be cleared hence. Those that follow come as a rush of energy and desire, desire not of the flesh, but of wisdom and truth. All becomes clearer to those who truly seek the way.

We, stand before thee and would be recognised as truth of what is. Each path comes to the what is? And along the way, we may choose. Do not fear these choices, as they embody the extension of wisdom. True wisdom is not narrow, it is all encompassing and would be known as such. No one truth is *the* truth, for each perceives truth from a different starting point. It is enough that they *see* truth.

We knock that you take action
We call that you may hear
We touch that you will sense
We show that you shall see and
We hold the hand that holds the pen

The river of earth, contains the seed of earth.
The river of man, contains the seed of man.

Thank you.

To Seek

Greetings – we gather. Come let us greet the day together. We travel as one with thee. We travel a straight path with all.

To question is wise. Does not the child ask many, many questions? And with each answer, a new question. Is this not how they learn? Fear not the questions, for each shall be answered in the course of things.

Is it not easier to trust in the known word, than to trust in the unknown? But which trust is the greater? If all is known, is there true need for trust? This does not require the abandon of seeking, for to seek what is ours and what is not, necessitates wisdom and wisdom is learned in trust and in each truth of self. Your truth may not be another's truth, but the essence of truth is in each and is essential to all that is good. In goodness we share, in goodness we grow. Giving of goodness is giving of self – without cause, without return. Is not this truth fraught with difficulty? But such an overcoming is rewarded in progress.

The motion is set in flow and this flow meanders, touching many as it goes on by. Watch child, do you not see the ripples, do they not bring results and so progress spreads its wings wide over all?

There is much to be taught and time to teach.

There is much to be learned and time to learn.

** *** **

When you take a leaf and renew its purpose, you halt the process of decay. So too the collected wisdom can halt the tide of decay and loss. The few are strong and may divert the many by wisdom, example and by love. Love is a powerful tool, if used wisely and in a selfless manner. Do not cling to love for it may suffocate, instead, open the arms forth, as love will stay when freed to choose.

Come now, let us tarry a little to frolic in the sun. Draw in the energy and peace to strengthen thy being. For both the body and soul blossom forth in the glow of light.

Golden light, white light –
Fill each being with joy and grace.
Fill each with power and growth.
Let each being know the why of your way
and let each one of these beings take up your glow.
Let each then go forth and share these gifts
with those about them,
that they in turn know and recognise –
Thy gift, and know the Giver
The giver of life and love.

And so it goes around.

Whispers

Good morning, child, what a clutter (*my painting bits and pieces*) – but out of chaos comes life. There is new life, even in your clutter. As you take up each item and exercise its purpose, so new life shall appear. Much of what is created may have no relevance to you but to another it shall be clear and concise in its appearance. Child, this is but the beginning of a long journey on which there may be detours, but learning shall be undertaken and all is in hand. The journey has begun and it is right to do so. Do you not feel the pulse of energy that surrounds you? Let us speak awhile.

Speak of silence and the peace that is held within the silence. There is a place where nature whispers on the wind, so as not to disturb the silence. But in the silence and within the whispers, there is much knowledge and love. You are not afraid to be alone. Do not fear the silence, as there is learning to behold.

Look to those who come to you and those to whom you are drawn. Look for the lesson each may hold. A word, a gesture, a knowing that will enlighten you. Yes, there is much about you to learn from. Not all lessons are in the print form and not all are shouted forth. Many messages are subtle in their presentation to you, however, the lesson is no less poignant.

Go in peace.

Sorrow

We are here, child of light. You need but speak and we attend.

Would you speak of sadness and sorrow? For it goes deep with many. Deep into their very being.

As in all things, there are lessons and the why of it is often veiled. Each must find or seek his own lesson and grow in the experience. It is often a length of time before we can actually face and see the lesson and some may miss this emphasis completely. Others seek too hard and long, and once again the learning is overlooked. Emotion is a wonderful sense, in its joy and sorrow, but do we not sometimes draw one more than the other to our place in time? It is as easy to draw the opposite, and to learn from both.

Do we not quickly learn from our mistakes and avoid these where possible? Why then can we not learn from our successes and triumphs? Why is pride and joy more difficult than pain and tears?

Again look to nature, she blooms regardless. She re-adjusts and blooms forth in the storm or in rain. After all, the sun shines and brings life forth. So too, you bring forth the light of joy and love into your life.

Now, let us look to the future. It is what you will, and it can be more but you cannot will for another. Each must be his own master of ceremonies orchestrating his own will, taking charge, taking responsibility, taking leave to be.

But in all of this we take care to wish no other harm, and to cause no other pain. Pain is a part of living in human form but it is the intention of harm we speak of.

Intention is a powerful tool and must be wielded carefully. Remember the tool may cut both ways, as does the sword of life. Again we return to choice, never choose to harm another either in thought or deed. To so choose, is to self harm. Who willingly puts their head on the block? Not I, M'Lord, not I.

Go now in peace and think on these words.

Joy Of Sharing

Good morning, child – let us speak of the joy of sharing. *(Meditation)*

You sit with another and share your space and time, and in the sharing you give of love. Giving is not measured as you may measure but measured indeed as all is recorded.

The Book of Records is maintained and indeed, you maintain the record as the self. For no other writes your record. A feather here, a stone there are each imprinted on the page. No deed of giving is too small for noting.

Come now, of *joy* we also speak. For to give or be given is to feel a sense of pure joy. You feel this joy, as do others, and the joy or the memory imprint remains along with thee, always. Arise and go forth and spread joy on thy path, that those who follow may gather the pebbles in their sack. Each holding firm a memory to be drawn forth in times of need, and joy must be recalled to life, for life's sake.

Hold forth a joy – a stone – feeling its size, its strength, its warmth and its energy; see its colour, its beauty, its shape and its purpose. Know its reason, its place and its time of existence.

For in all life, there is purpose to existence, sometimes obscure, but know that purpose is paramount to all life forms, seen and unseen. We digress! Go forth this day in the joy of giving, and receive joy as given.

Promise

Good morrow – much is accomplished in the hours of sleep and when the time is right this knowledge will be to hand. A small example is to the understanding you have of waiting for the right moment, the trust in knowing that when the time is right all shall be revealed. But until then a little at a time is how the work progresses.

In the time of aloneness there is growth for all and from this growth comes life anew.

New life holds promise, it is untarnished and pure. Treasure it well. A life, or a bud, holds the energy of the universe within. Nurture this gift and guard it well, for life in any form is precious.

Go now and think awhile.

Vigilance

Good morning – a new day dawns afresh and in the stillness is the sound of life.

All upon the earth are related and yet it is forgotten that one is connected to the other. In the destruction of this connection we destroy the self. It must be plain to all to avoid such disastrous acts, and yet much is taken for granted. They assume that all will be well, regardless of their deeds.

Too often the intention is worthy but the deed is contrary. We must strive to bring the two into harmony and balance, as must all others; quite a feat you might say. However, consider the worth of such an endeavour. Peace and harmony in all things. To man this seems inconceivable and yet is there not hope for just such an outcome? Does not every fibre of life yearn for such as this?

To achieve such as this, is to live purely and simply in one's own truth. Be true to thy own self and to all others true acceptance. Query not their deeds, only thy own. Find the balance, not swinging left or right, but holding to the centre. Hold to what you know to be truth, knowing that it is within, as a beacon in the mist held steady and high for all to see and trust.

Be guided by this lamp and be watchful as the mist parts. In the parting is wisdom and understanding, and such will be there for those who keep vigil. Know this and know that it is nigh.

In peace and harmony.
Amen

Distance

Hello, child. We are here and would speak with you in the time available. Time is not so important. A few moments here and there are all that we require, for a great deal may be achieved in a short distance. A distance does not require physical expenditure, it may be distance travelled by the hand of time, one moment or one circle of the face, or indeed many such circles. For now we shall share one or more of such circles of distance

Is not humour a wonderful rejuvenator of life and energy? We should not be so serious so often. Let humour and laughter enter this domain. The domain child, is the whole of thy being, the whole of each being, and such sacred domains must be cherished and nurtured, and laughter is essential in this process of care.

The process of care spreads outward from the self, but only and when the self is truly nurtured and in fine balance. If we venture outward in a state of unbalance, we cannot truly nurture the self or any other. We may in fact fail the self and/or others. If we cannot judge truly when we are out of balance, then decisions in this state may be unwise and unwarranted. Take care of the self and, by example, the care extends to others about thee. All then, is well.

Give the gift of knowledge to the children,
that they may make of it what thy will.

Inner Peace

Good morning. We are with you. Times of peace are rare. You and those about you need to find and nurture this state of inner peace. All that is required may be achieved if one is in the state of true peace and harmony, with the One. All life radiates from the centre and if this centre is in chaos, the radiation is hazardous. The eddies must circle gently outwards from the centre, maintaining a calming balance to the self and to those in near proximity. Each aspect creates a response and the needed response at present is calming – peace and harmony.

Peace and chaos must maintain balance, for the joy of life to be truly appreciated and known. Find the middle and bathe in the joy. There are times when this seems a difficult task, but discipline and training help the process of knowing, and these together lead to understanding. Try and recollect a time or times of a quick or sudden flash of understanding, when every piece fell into place in *the* instant. This is what one aims for in life, this clarity of thought, and of place. Do you recall such an instance when the thought and the place collided at the right moment in time? Is it not a grand knowing, that allows the feeling, the perception of the senses to glow and to thus radiate to all, near and far? The glow of the energy from within at such a moment is as a beacon to all. The knowing and the unknowing ones are for a moment touched by the radiance of your pure moment of understanding.

There is so much to share with others and often this sharing is offered in ignorance. A gesture, a look, a word, each of these may be a 'sharing' and yet we may be ignorant of the reception this gift is given. A good moment may be given, it may be received, and each in itself is a treasure to behold. For that which is given without fanfare is indeed a true treasure of love, a love, which is unshackled, a love that makes no claim.

Find the peace within.

Sincerity

Greetings. Now for today – let us speak of peace and sincerity. All actions should be accompanied by sincerity of deed. If this cannot be applied to the deed then another path or action should prevail. True sincerity of action shall result in peace and with this peace, contentment of spirit in a deed well done.

There are times child, when a deed may appear to be a burden, but perhaps the burden is a lesson in disguise. But then you ask, how to differentiate? If we are in tune with the self the power of intuition will dominate and we may discern the lesson.

There is so much that one carries, some of which may be safely set down now. It is like an everyday task, when it is complete the tools are put away safely until they are required again. So too that which we carry may in turn be set aside, or if needs be carried a little further. Do not, however, carry that which is not required of thee. This again is a time to look squarely at the deed or the 'burden', and in sincerity, make the choice with guidance from the inner self – the intuitive knowing.

Each journey begins with a step and often a number of journeys may work in unison or perhaps they parallel one another. One task may, and often does, incorporate another or, indeed, many others. Weaving, always weaving, one with another or one within another. Such patterns add to the wonder of things.

Does not the wonder bring a flowing sense of peace to all? That it flows over and around thee in sheer abundance creates the peace desired within the self. This sense of peace and contentment may then flow onto others and it does in more ways than can be imagined.

Trust the self, trust the intuitive knowing and all shall be well with thee. For in trust lies true peace and harmony with all.

Book Of Records

Dear child, we are here with thee now and always. Open thy heart and mind to all that is about thee. The very air you breathe, the sounds you hear, for in all there is life and love. Even the smallest, the seemingly most insignificant item of your daily life is of note, and in itself of value. Who so ever shall note this item is blessed. It is not always the big, the large, the enormous item or event, that is the most needed or important. Look also to the small and seemingly insignificant. Remember to balance the needs both small and large. Do not strive only for attention. Remember all is listed in the Book of Records and it is the self that writes upon the page. Be true to the self, be true to thy way.

Fear not the shadows of life upon thy way, as the light of love shines forth for thee. Go ahead in love and light. We walk with thee in all.

Listen

Hello, child. Yes, we would speak. Speak of this and that and indeed of much more. Would you listen?

Oh Yes!

All will be clear in time and you will know which decision to make, for there is much to do and you shall do it.

What?

No, No! Not yet. However, all will be clear in time. Enjoy the now and treasure these moments. Each moment is as a pearl, it is precious. Gather and treasure each one in turn.

Actions

Dear one. The cloud rests gently on the soul as it dissipates to nothingness. Fear not the consequences of your actions, all is well. Those who care are never far from thee. Space, time and distance is as nothing to those who gather here.

Remember that for every movement there is a counter movement, so be aware of the purpose in action, or indeed in *no* action. We do not always need to act, silence and inaction may be the necessary requirement.

In stilling the self and remaining in balance, one can perceive the correct requirements for the specific decision – to take action or to be still. In the silence we speak, and can be heard if help is required, but know that you are never just one alone. We, you and I are many. We have been many for now and in eons past. There is much to do at this time in the universe, and many gather, not so many as could, but even a few may be as many with guidance and love. Love is indeed a powerful tool, use it wisely, and do not abuse this tool. Remembering movement goes both ways and often the rebound punches harder than the original push or deed.

Our frailty is sometimes disguised as aggression and power. Be aware of frailty and adjust for the circumstances. Do not fear your weaknesses but be aware of them and counter them with love, not aggression and power. There is no shame in weakness and it is often from the control or conquering of same that we grow in self and in love. There is weakness in all, as it balances with our strength. Learn to adapt, learn to adjust, and learn to love all of the self in its glory and in its pain. For does this not maketh thee whole? And the whole in harmony is a force indeed.

Go now and take joy in the silence – seeking silence for thy whole being is as a gift to thee.

Everything Speaks

I will try to be gentle and to walk with dignity in all that I do. With guidance I shall try to select and use words of joy and love, knowing they cannot be retrieved once spoken. Help me to avoid causing pain.

In everything child, we speak to thee. As a dove flies, as a cloud passes, as the wind blows, we are in everything that touches the heart, even thy pain. We are as one in all and know thy all. We are with thee, and thee, and thee.

The road may be long or short, but in either the traveller is not alone. Too often we fear the silence and the space of peace. Aloneness is not to be feared, it is to be rejoiced and utilised. Aloneness gives one time to re-centre, re-energise, re-focus and re-live. To live the moment and to embrace its joys – the grace it brings to thee. Yet, so often we let it slip past unattended and unadorned. It is lost.

Look not back at what is lost. Seek only what is at hand and reach out in trust and love to take hold. It may burn, it may sting but *look*, what is it you *hold?* For it is yours, to do with, what you may and it is yours for a reason. Brush not the moment aside, it is your life, your destiny, your immediate knowing.

Do you need to learn how to recognize joy? Too often we recognise only the pain.

Thank you.

Why Analyse?

Good morning dear friends. We speak at all times to as many as may hear, but few truly listen. It is as simple as listening to one's own thoughts, but then they begin to analyse. Catch the thoughts as they flow by. Like a fisherman – net them and draw them to the surface, that you may inspect them and be pleased. Do you analyse the fish? No! you look at it, identify it and enjoy the pleasure of the catch, and the thought of sharing its energy in a meal. If it is too small you send it back, as you may do with a small developing thought.

On the lake is there not silence? The gentle lapping of the water at your feet. The gentle sound of this movement, not interrupting the peace, only enhancing the moment. The sun flashes across the water, deceiving and delighting the eye. The smell of the earth and life about you frees the senses to soar. You are relaxed and at peace. Feel the peace and know thy whole being. Feel the breath of life within and about you, as life caresses your being. Sense the beauty and the peace in this silent space. The birds, the wind, the gentle movement of the water at your feet, add to your inner silence. You are still. Be still and just BE. Be in the moment, be in the now. Open the mind and let the thoughts fly free. Watch them and trawl only the larger ones and only those of use for this moment. Life - Love - Light! What more do you need, child? If you have these, then you have also trust in the self and in the universal wisdom.

Go, live life, in love and light.

Thank you.

Service

Dear child, service is in each breath that you take. Often we look to the large avenues of service and do not realize that the very small deed, a breath, a smile or even our presence in a room, may be of service to others. The needs of those about us are as of our needs and they are often just a small gesture, an acknowledgement of being.

However, there is much to do and the smaller gestures set the ripples and patterns in progress. Each small ripple reaches out to another and to yet another, forming the patterns of life's needs now acknowledged. Each of these small ripples form together to create a larger pattern that spreads out into the universe, sending light back to the source of the small deed. Know that even the smallest deed is noted. Remembering that the small effort is of no less importance than the large effort. It is in the attitude and the intention that there is grace and light.

Service, child, is in being true to the self and in sharing this truth with those about you. This truth is often difficult to define, as we rarely look to the self and question the self. It is easier to look to others and question their truths. Look also to the self and then just be. For in being we share the self with those about us. Do not ponder on this, as the self knows what is within and it shines forth on occasions of need and of joy. Even in pain the self shines forth, but we in pain lose sight of the reason and of the lesson. Then later we may recall, if we choose and see the way of things.

** *** **

Blue feather drifting, sees all.
Floating on the substance of wind it flies free.
Where shall it rest and with whom?
Float free, child, as the feather.
Trust the wind and know that thou art safe,
On the breath of the Lord the one and all.

Go now in peace. We are with you in all things.

Daily Life

Yes, child, we are here. We have waited for this moment, as you have been busy with life. Now as you are still, we may speak with thee. Life must go on and it may seem an encumbrance to carry out the duties of life, but we are ever patient and will always be.

Life may cloud the mind but in the quiet spaces there is peace to be found. You do not need to search, it waits and when found you know. The knowing is in the moment and the moment is full. Everything responds to the moment of knowing the silence, the peace – a deep peace within and around you – the senses, the intuitive sense. Every part of the being is alive and in that moment you know. You know the all of things. In a busy life, these moments seem few and far, they seem scattered and difficult to perceive, but in the silence they wait to be discovered and to be explored.

Find time in life to still the mind, the heart and the body – then peace shall be all encompassing. Peace shall be yours.

Self-Care

We welcome you, child, it is a good morning. Draw in the breath of the morning, clear thy mind and refresh thy soul. Feel the fresh breeze of the new day caress thy skin as it cools thee. Do not rush at your work as there is, and will be, time to address the enquiries of others.

We must address our own needs first. We have a duty and a responsibility to care for the self – not only in the physical sense of need each day but also in the spiritual sense. For are these our needs, of less importance? A plant left unattended may struggle for life, and may even wither and die. So too the unattended self struggles for its very existence. Tend the inner one as you should, and as you do, tend the outer body. Spoil and care for each, as they are one with each other and to separate or to ignore part, is to slowly destroy both. Balance. Then in balance we may reach out to others. *Not before.*

Too often those on the earth plain reach out to others offering help and support, when they themselves are ailing. This support can only be temporary, as both beings are in a state of imbalance. To be true to both and to truly offer help we must heal the self first. There is time to reach out; there is a time to reach out but for both to be safe and remain whole, the carer likewise must be whole. Each being has a duty of care to the self and each being is a part of the whole. The duty of care is not to carry more than is required. Carry only your own load. Those about you must carry their own.

This is not to say that when a being's load is lightened he or she may, walking beside a friend, ease the friend's load. Mind, ease it, and *not* take it. For you each carry your own lessons and your own knowledge.

Know this and remember, caring for the self is a divine duty and should indeed be an earthly pleasure. Take pleasure in the self, in the whole of the self. Then take pleasure in those about you. Have you and those about you not noticed, that in caring for the self in truth, others learn and take heart?

Do not ignore the self.

Go in light and love and care for the self.
Remember it is your duty and a life task.

Change

Greetings.

Yes, child, it is time to plant the new seeds and the soil awaits. Child of light enjoy your special day as we enjoy being with you.

The decisions of late have been hard but you fail no one. They must move on, as you must. There is so much newness about, if only people would to look. Too often we seek safety and entrapment of our own making, rather than newness and growth.

Safety represents security. Newness to many represents change and the fear they associate with change. Fear not change, for as life circles about you there is always newness. Just reach out and grab a hold. Catch the golden ring as the carousel turns.

Dear friends why have I been so angry and distracted this week? Is it these changes? Is it fear of the unknown?

Bingo! You win the prize. You each have fear built into your makeup it is meant as a warning devise but when allowed a free hand to rule it is a power unleashed. Hold fear in check. Why is it people unleash fear but hold joy in tight check? Try the reverse and enjoy the outcome. You may and will be quite surprised. Unleash your joy. You give it to others, can you not give it to yourself?

Now, child, go into the day in our love and light, and in the love and light that is your own. Remembering always we are all of the One. The I am presence within and without, in and about all.

You are loved — you are love.

Take Hold Of Life

Good morning, child, time is not important. What is important is to take hold of life and live it. Sit with us now and quietly go to the inner realm. Feel the peace. Know this peace, that in times of stress you may recognise and recall it. Relaxation of mind and spirit is important for in a relaxed state, time may be better used. When the mind and body are unduly stressed time is mismanaged, and opportunities may be overlooked or lost. Undue stress also puts the health at risk.

Make time to sit quietly, either alone or with others. Clear the mind of stress and of duty, and then set the imagination free. Then watch as the imagination roams unrestricted. Do not let the sounds of life distract the free thoughts. Do not allow the distraction to develop a sense of anger and frustration within you. Instead flow with the distraction, allowing it to be moulded to your stream of thought. Thus you become one with thought and sound. You become free. This is your time to seek peace, to do and create as you wish in your imagined world. It is in this free world that you may sow the seeds of future successes and pleasures. Send out your desires, remembering that what you send out may indeed come to you – do you truly want it?

Confused

I am in a state of flux. It seems as if everything is standing still as I rush by, and yet I don't appear to be moving at all. I feel confused and angry but I cannot come to an understanding of why. Dear friends I have no reason for feeling like this as I am and have been very blessed over the years. Will you speak with me now and help me to know myself? The self I hid so long ago. I have a need to know her.

Dear child, confusion surrounds many, it is life and all of its venues. But, you know the peace that comes with balance. You need only to find the balance again. You feel it already as you write. In the writing, as in meditation or stillness, you find the peace. Stand still, things are afoot, but you have no need to rush at them. What is, is, and it comes in good time. When the time is right for progress, so you shall progress along your way. But, remember, stillness is part of progressing.

It is the period of preparation. Child, we must be prepared and it is so with you, and with those about you. This is the time of preparation and rest. All is well, hold fear off, as there is no need of fear. Hold confusion off as this may lead to fear and it has no place here.

For now, just enjoy each day and the experience each new day brings forth. Learn from the new and the experiences of the now. Fill your mind and heart with peace and love and know all is in hand.

The future often seems a mystery, but every moment of the now builds the future. Like bricks in a path, we lay one at a time and step forward one step at a time. The bricks are being laid and when rested you shall step forward in grace and in love. Know always we step and rest with thee.

We see the fear and confusion in your world, and we would have it melt away but it is in each, as you, to create this peace and tranquillity. Do it not, by struggling but by silence and un-abandoned love.

Imagine

Dear one, there is much about and it is felt by many, many more than your immediate circle. Mother earth shakes herself, as a dog shakes off the fleas and little irritation, to roll in the sand and then shake from the head to the tail, rolling the muscles of the whole body. And so the earth's ripples spread outward to many. There is an unsettling, a period of making ready, but for what, many ask? Fear not for preparations are well in hand.

Does it not remind one of the impatience and curiosity of the child? Too soon you lose sight of the child, but the child clings to the sight of you. The child is ever present and guards the wonder of things. You have only to ask, you have only to look, and it is the imagination that opens this gateway to wonder. Will you not reach out and open it – reconnect with the inner self?

In the imagination we can create our hearts desire and who is to say we cannot then manifest this desire? Why don't you try it? Many have and with great success. Imagine it, draw it, and bring it to you. However, bring it with unconditional love, no ties. Experiment child and have fun. Bring laughter to your life and all else shall follow. Laughter frees the soul to experience joy – pure joy.

Go in peace and seek the laughter.

Look

Dear child, still the self. Still the mind, that you may open to all. All that is about thee, the light and shade, the day and night, the wind, the air, the breath you breathe. All in life may guide and teach thee. There are in life many teachers, not only in the human form. We can learn much from one another and from life about us. Look child! Look about you, using not only the eyes but all of the senses. Feel the wisdom about you, for it is held within many aspects of life. Ask of nature what it can show you and share with you, for it has much to share and would do so, if given the opportunity

Divest yourself and move forward, ridding the self of that which is unnecessary. You have started the clearing process and when it is complete, then you will know your way. Trust, and in time, all shall be clear. Have you not waited so long? Can you not wait a little longer?

Go now, do as the day needs and know there are surprises in store – of a great nature.

The Child

Child of light, we do not see you as a child. We see the person and the child within, as we do with all. Too often the child fades from your sight. Therefore we wish only to call it back into focus.

There is much we can learn from children and from the child within, but we must reach deep into hidden areas of the heart and in some instances, from the locked areas of the mind. To awaken, the child needs only the freedom of the imagination, freedom with love, no restrictions, no boundaries. Let the thoughts and feelings flow free, then watch where they meander.

There is so much pleasure in free thought, and all children have this gift. How often have you to call, or recall a child from its game, from the intensity of its thoughts? 'Just a minute', they reply, for in truth they need time to come back to *reality*. The child's world is so vast, and it is a world that you are invited to reclaim. It is from that world that you may manifest your desires. Reach into it in innocence and love, and create your dreams in the now.

It may take time and practice, but, once again, join with the child and become as one in the balance of things.

To Each

Often, when seeking, some move ahead a little too fast. Each new step, each new direction should be measured, as to all information. Information should be pursued and weighed. If it is found wanting then it needs to be discarded. Keep only to the self that which holds truth in its essence. Guide those you teach, and temper their enthusiasm with moderation and patience. Have you not suffered many lessons in patience? So too must they.

All shall share in learning and wisdom. Share knowledge, for each follows different pathways and the knowing will guide, not distract from the worth of each. Some fear that to share means a loss, but NO, it means growth.

To share is to grow in wisdom and love. Each has his own way to follow. We cannot do all that we learn and are acquainted with, but the learning opens our way to clear knowledge and a deeper understanding of the way of things.

** *** **

Do not fear the changes about you –
all will be made clear in time.

Open your heart to the seed of wisdom –
and look to those who are drawn to you.

Seekers need guidance –
guide with love and care.
Guide in gentleness –
and walk proudly.

Aspect

Dear child, when the heart is heavy, go within and draw out the pain. Open the heart to love. Love is to be nurtured, not feared. Love is in all that surrounds you. You are love. Rejoice in the love of life itself.

At times like these we feel we are adrift, but the time is measured and progress follows. These periods of rest and quiet should be treated as just that, and you should take advantage of the quiet time.

Each aspect of life has its place in the order of things and from each aspect we learn, if we choose to do so. Learning comes to those who see it. Just as the child continuously asks, 'Why?' so too must we. Seek learning in all things and in each day. Learning comes in many forms and each is precious in its own right. Hold always to the self that you may have choices, even in learning.

Go now child and be about your day.

Share the words with those who would listen. For in this too we learn – you and I together.

Informal

We are here child and would spend time with you now and throughout each day. We are always about and would have you know this. The morning air is fresh and the day glows in life. We who gather take in this glow and become one with it. So too must you. Be of the day and be in the day. Be as one with all about thee.

Our words may at times seem strange but, in time, clarity comes to thee. Do not close the mind and the heart, for life shall pass unlived. Open to that which is and be part of the knowing. Be as one with all in that knowing. Do not fear the unknown for it is just a state not yet attained. That which is needed shall be known. By opening to learning and then by practice, knowing shall be attained. That which is needed shall be provided to thee. In opening to that which is around thee, so ye shall learn and be, as needs be.

In the wider scheme of things you have a place. You shall experience and learn, that you may then share this learning with others. All of your life has been learning, to bring you to this point in time and the learning continues daily, formally and informally. Often the formal lessons overshadow the informal but do not discount the informal, as this often comes from personal experience or in the form of information from others. Again, this learning may come from a person or from nature. Be open to the lessons of informal learning. Do not rush about with the eyes and ears closed. Open each of the senses each day and absorb all you can. You may be surprised just how much you can learn this way.

The method of formal learning teaches us the rules of learning or gaining wisdom. Informal methods of learning teach us by experience. Experience is a great teacher and a great leveller of wisdom and its practice.

Truth and love – a base to work out from.

A Grain Of Sand

Yes, child, we await you and would gather in your day. There is so much to do and yet, little by little, each grain must be studied and known, for nothing is too small. Everything has significance in the scheme of things, as do you and those about you.

The time draws near when you shall be of significance, when you must step forward in your way. To the now, there has been much learning and preparation and the significance of these shall be known. For some the purpose may be grand, for others a small deed, but each is as important as the next. No one is greater than the other and to think so, is foolish.

There is peace about you child, a peace that may rest upon many. This peace moves outward as the smoke from a candle, touching others as it passes. Each in turn may feel and experience the peace if they but open to all. There is in all a centre of light that links each to the other, but few remember this light source. It is time now to awaken the light source within, that they may know and teach the way to others. It is to be done in the way of peace and love, and in gentleness and trust. Light does not force its way upon the many, but is there waiting to be let in. They just need to lift the shutters or to open the heart. So simple – to go within and find their own love, the source of their light. Go within, trust the self, trust the One and the connection to all things. Acknowledge the connection and be as one with all.

* *** **

Many have moved away too far, too fast. Now they must stop and rest. Now they seek guidance and love, but each must start within themselves, then work outwards. To work outward without the inner self, is to sail a boat without the sail. It flounders, you flounder. Each must take strength from the inner depths of knowledge and recognise the *love they are.* In recognising this truth we may then move outward and be as a connection and guide, that others may take note and seek the way to self-fulfilment, enlightenment and truth.

In each is light and love, and in these we are at peace with all. Without light and love, or in fear of light and love, we turn our backs on peace and dwell in chaos. Awaken and share the joy of love, the being with light and the true sense of peace, with those about us. It is so simple a task that many see not. Just be. Be as the self in truth. Be as the one in light, and be to all in truth and love. Then peace shall be to all, as light is to day.

There is, child, an abundance of true love, if we but look within and acknowledge the concept of love. Why is this so hard? Why do we want and seek outwardly what each truly has within? Love the self and love shall surround all. Remember the flowers by the way, they bloom and grow in trust, for they are of the one and accept this knowing. It is only we who question, and it is the self we question most. Can we not accept and love the self in its image of life and love – as it is?

Let fear drop away. Let anxiety drop away. Let ignorance drop away and be the one you are. Be the connection that you are and know, and acknowledge, the self for who you are – *now*, in this time of joy and love.

** *** **

Be a part of your own being and acknowledge that being, as must all, for we are the All and in this recognition lies harmony. Feel the harmony flowing through, around and outward, from your being. Be the harmony and be of the harmony. Reach in, reach out and be.

There is so much for each to do and you may work as one or as many, but in the doing you work as one in all, and it shall be done in love.

Peace comes to those who seek it. Love come to those who seek it and then each overflows to those who sleep in ignorance. The power of harmony reaches out to all and, in the movement, it is hard to ignore. It touches many and will not be ignored. Demonstrate the self to others in gentle and loving ways. Be at peace with the self and vibrate the colour of love and light as you pass each day by. This vibration will help the sender and the receiver as in all. As in the One within all.

Reach in, reach out and give to the self and of the self. Give in light and love, and know thy way, remembering each day brings blessings. Each day holds joy. Do not overlook the now and live in love, for this is to truly live. In truly living as the self, we give to others.

It is done, go about the day.

Three

Good Friday – today we shall work as three, but do not see this in the sense of limitation. Three is the number of power and of love. For one without the other creates imbalance. To the power of three we add love and thus life itself, in forms yet unimagined. For many see life in only that which breaths the air and yet there is life in many realms.

** *** **

Easter Sunday – such a day as has dawned. We bid welcome to the light of love, and welcome you upon the plain of joy. The depths of love well up to encompass all in its surge of energy. This day brings love to all, for is it not a day of rejoicing and renewal?

Come, as we gather together, join hands about the world in peace and love. Share in the beauty of the day and the infinite moment in which all existence is. Behold the one who greets all in splendour and light. For is it not a day of days, when hands may reach out to all others in peace? Take a moment to breathe in this peace, that it may share and be shared amongst all creatures of the way.

** *** **

The way is ahead for those who seek it, look not back in dread but in the joy that has brought each to this moment in time.

ALL is within time and time is within all. Time is not our enemy, but a friend who shares willingly each precious moment. We envisage time as an enemy. Time is but an energy that we may utilise, if we so wish, to our advantage. Or indeed we may just flow peacefully with it. Do not try to go against it. Work with time, not for it and do not let the clock rule you.

Time may be likened to an incredibly beautiful thought experienced in a split second, and yet when unfolded to a friend it may take 10 or 15 minutes to describe.

Time is your friend.
Use it well and it shall serve you well.

Pathway

Greetings, there are many ways to the enlightened one. Each path is, in its way, the correct path for the seeker at the time. We do not all crowd one way. For each individual knows his or her way, be it hidden at times. Some struggle harder than others, but it is by choice, for the learning that is required.

Trust your instincts, trust your senses and your inner knowing. Go the way you feel is most comfortable. All learning is good, based on what you take from the experience. We each gather to the self that which we truly need. That, which is excess falls away if unattended, and this is correctly so. Let the excess fall away; do not carry that which is irrelevant.

Circling ever outward, the snowdrop falls and is seen, then it is absorbed and becomes as the other. Energy and life flow from each crystal clear drop. The rainbows gather within each flake to share their energy and colour with the universe. The circle moves outward in an ever-continuing motion of energy.

Those who gather, bring different energies and colours, to mingle and share with those about, circling, ever circling, and thus growing in strength and wisdom. That which is, is. But those who gather, are sometimes in ignorance of the strength of love contained within their energy sphere. But they shall know, step by step, as they move forward and become aware.

** *** **

Awareness appears to come only in times of pure peace, or in times of despair, but it will come also in times of balance. We need only to heed the desire for balance and nurture this energy, each finding this special knowing, this sense of self as one, as part of the whole.

Within the quad you have the square, the circle and the triangle. You have the directions and the seasons, you have power and energy within the seed. Nurture well in gentleness and love, allow it to open and bloom in its own time. For with the opening and the maturity comes forth many seeds to scatter in the four ways of nature 4 is to 8, is to 12, is to the circle of all ways. As in nature, look to its lessons and learn well the ways of being, as with the One in harmony.

As with the quad, so too the nucleus is the centre, the seed. No one is the centre, but each sends out love from their centre. Send forth love freely upon the way, in that each has power and so too, peace. Share freely, do not hold only to the self. Scatter forth the seeds of love and joy, allowing those who will to gather as they may.

The Journey

Dear friends I am here.

As are we child. That which you experience at night in your dream space shall be made clear in due course. The doors have opened and you have walked through, taking in all that you require to thus open the channels of recall. All is hidden within upon the soul map and each path you trace becomes illuminated and clear.

To take a journey of significance we must first read the map and find the direction. Do not rush into this journey unprepared.

There is beauty all around, just as there is beauty in each one of you. Too often, we see not the beauty. Always take time child to see the beauty and to draw it into you. There is no quota on the beauty we may draw to ourselves or that we send to those about us by our deeds and in our ways of gentleness and care. Be to others as to the self, that they may be part of the journey to harmony. It is time to realise the significance of being and to take responsibility for each day and for each moment within it. We are not perfect, nor do we ask to be, but we must try to be that which we truly know we may be.

There is nothing that we cannot achieve, if we step forward in trust and with purpose. It is just a matter of taking the step. One leads to two, leads to three and so on, until we may run free, free of guilt and fear. Free of binds and woes, we may go forward and grow in light and love.

** *** **

Then having made the choice, we are bound to share this knowing freely with the self and with others. With the *self* I hear you say? Yes. Take in that which is and share generously with the self, in that you do not deny or shutter the inner knowing, instead opening up to that which is.

Bathe in the knowing, rollick in the joy and then when you have your fill, go forth and share this pure joy with any who are free to listen. Give generously but do not force the way, as some are not yet ready to take note. Just drop a seed or two and pass. When the time is right the seed shall sprout forth of its own volition. Remember that many seeds lay dormant, season after season, but with the rain of joy they open and send forth their shoots of life. To lay still over many seasons is but to wait for the right moment, and you may be long gone from this point of sowing. You may be busy elsewhere, but the seed shall come forth to life at the appointed moment, and you do not need to see each of these moments. Just know and trust that they shall occur in the time decreed.

For today, there is much to do. Open your mind and heart and share the joy within, as we share ours with you. Go forth upon the day and note the beauty of the moment. Be as one with all that surrounds you. Feel and know the way of life, the life that courses within and without, in the colours, the odours, the touch that awakens a memory on a page in the book of knowing. Do you not feel the energy in the very air about you, the excitement, the pleasure and the joy? All of this is *LOVE*. The love of all, the love of self, the love of life. The being with all, in all and with the One in all.

** *** **

Connect and be connected to all that you may. For this is to truly give – to and of the self in all that we do. Reach out and touch that which is.

We are one, we are many. For now the lessons continue and the knowledge grows. In time proof shall be forth coming, not necessarily for the self but for those who may question – they shall have their proof, and in the proof is their freedom to again trust in love.

Go, enjoy the journey.

Harmony

Good morning, child, be guided ever by your intuition and know that in all you are protected. Just be, for there is nothing that you must do at present.

> Be, just be –
> be as you are.
> And all shall be
> revealed as needs – be.

Harmony rests easy in this place and many shall drink of this harmony, taking it forth to share with those they know. Is this not what we hope for, that the harmony of life spread outward returning all to the knowledge harmony enfolds? Child, all is at hand, you have but to be as the self and get on with your way.

Come, now let us look to that which is most eminent, the why of things. Do we not work to this end? Do we not work toward being as one with all? Too often, we forget to be. From childhood we ask, 'Why?' And this in turn brings knowing and the understanding of why something is as it is. So to the search for truth and love, for are these not of the One? And the search continues throughout our lifetimes. The why of all is within and each answer is encased within our very being. It is the searching outward that confuses and confounds the seeker.

Find the stillness and you find the why of things. Then you need only the how and when, but these shall be evident in the why. All is as it should be. Trust this knowing and go within to seek your answers, as must each individual.

In the search for answers we seek and find growth and understanding. This is as must be. For in growth and understanding we find the self, and come to know the being of self. This then, acknowledged and accepted, leads us to the why, and so too, the circle of wisdom is enclosed, enfolding that which is within.

Do not be confused, as in all learning, clarity comes with time and practice. Each new learning exercise enfolds the practice and in such we progress upon our path with our considerable realisation. Sometimes we have not been aware of *the journey*, just suddenly of our arrival. Is this then not a joyous occasion, one to be celebrate and shared with those about us?

Now, go and celebrate.

Found

Child, take your pen and write gently the words we give. For it is in the giving that we join with all and this joining facilitates the learning process. You are not lost, you are found and in the finding, you step ahead. That which seems now to be confusing shall soon clear, for you have made it so. You have cleared the path ahead and as such you shall grow in the glory of wisdom. Such shall be your way.

Many shall follow such a way, but each comes to the way by various means and wisdoms. Wisdom is vast in its path of glory and each reads this wisdom in their chosen way. One should not criticise or berate another, as each comes to their way in their own chosen time and in their own chose manner.

Some pathways may be clear but others are pitted and need negotiation. However, the traveller shall arrive at the appointed or agreed time. This does not prevent one from learning and sharing all that they may along their way, as the learning and sharing may help others in their journey.

Confounded

So too we go ahead, that we may lead and smooth the way. As we move ahead others walk beside and, yet again, others follow. For each who walk the path of life are well cared for and, indeed, have many companions upon their way. Too often, we fear or perceive a journey of 'alonement' but to know and trust in the self is to know and trust the way, and those who travel along this way in procession with us. We are never alone, not even when we sense or perceive that we are lost. One is never lost, just occasionally confused or confounded by circumstance and life.

So too we work in joyous harmony with those we serve and greet upon the way. It is this joyful band of workers who may bring harmony and love again to life. Each of you, regardless of task or indeed the size of the task, shall, in your finding of wisdom, bring joy and love to the lives of these about you and of those who brush by you in the daily passing of time and life. Many merely brush by in the taking of wisdom but this, at that time, for them is sufficient. For within that moment of their life many such occurrences may be unfolding.

It is difficult for us to perceive just what may, and is possible to, occur within a moment of time, remembering that we operate on numerous levels at one time, and not just on one level. There is the mind, the heart, the soul, the senses and the being – not as separate parts, but as a whole, each operating together for the benefit of the one, the self.

When the self thus operates as a whole in unison, such shall be achieved as to overwhelm the one and in these moments; we know and sense the joy of this knowing. What is, is, and in many ways we come to this knowing and to that sense of achievement, in the moment of knowing.

Enough, now go into your day and enjoy being!

Acknowledgement

Child, it is always a pleasure to be acknowledged, here and there it notes our very being. Each in their own way desires acknowledgement, but often it comes in a manner least expected and from a source that had not been intimate or known. We do not all do deeds to seek acknowledgement, but when it is offered freely it is, and should be, accepted with grace and dignity.

Clouds

Dear child, the clouds that are about you will soon clear, and all is and shall be well with thee. It has been a long journey and all need to rest after such a journey. You are resting and this is as it should be.

This period shall pass and all that is required of this time shall be achieved. Often when there is change about we feel it only in one area of our being. However, with growth and development, be aware of this change in all aspects of your being. Not knowing which to acknowledge, you have become confused, but as you develop, you shall bring each aspect into harmony with the other, and so read from the whole. You will no longer need to read or recognise the aspects of your being as individual parts.

The more intuitive we become, or rather the more aware of our intuitive abilities we become, the more powerful we become in our personal unity. In uniting all of our aspects we reunite with the universe in all of its powers. We are able to absorb this energy as a whole being, one who is re-connected with the *All*. For some the connection is never in doubt, for others, life distances us from the knowledge of the connection.

** *** **

The connection itself is never broken or lost; we just lose sight of the knowledge. Then when we again commence our search, the knowledge seems overwhelming and this is because, at his point, we need patience and guidance.

You cannot expect to walk into a library and absorb the information in each book upon the instant, and yet when we seek the way this is often what we expect.

Although the information is within, to have it *all* recalled at one instant would overload and damage the previously sleeping being. Each being is precious, and is thus guarded and guided through this process of re-opening to the All That Is.

All that is required by the being shall be revealed and for many at this time it is well afoot. There is much that shall be known, and in the knowing, much that shall be done. For is it not the way of things?

The Way Ahead

Dear friends I am here and I seek your company.

It is ever given, child of woman, gladly and with love. When we last communed, we spoke of acknowledgement, growth and pathways. So to it is done and we shall move ahead to speak of the way ahead. It is generally smooth and profitable, not just in the one sense of profit, but in every sense of the word.

You and your life, and outward also to those about you, shall profit from life, from wisdom and from joy. There is so much that awaits you, hold out your hand and take hold of the future in the now. Grasp it and grow with it.

Each of us must face our fears and step through them, for they are but illusions. They may seem real enough at the time, but take courage and know thy way is clear. You may choose whichever path you wish, knowing we travel it with you. At this time no way is wrong, the choice is yours to make, knowing that your choice is the right choice. For there is work to do, wherever you may be, and it shall be done.

As in chess there are moves and counter moves, and now on a clear board, you may make your move. Go in any direction you wish. It is but for you to go in faith and with trust. Open your heart, child, and your wish shall be granted.

There is magic within and about you. Go, be one with it and bring magic to the lives of those you meet. You shall do this because you are you, and because it is your way. Light the hearts, light the minds and light the way ahead, not only for thyself but for many others. You can do this and we are there ever with thee. No task is worked in isolation, either for you or for others. *Know this to be truth.*

Choose your path, it need not be a wise choice – as it is but a choice and now is the time to make a choice. Just do it. All shall be well.

Choice

Greetings – the light within and around you becomes stronger as you become more attuned to the knowing, the inner self. That of which we are all a part, as one in the One. So too, at this time, the energies and vibrations of the earth are being raised.

It is time now to awaken the sleeping ones, but in all things there are choices. For those who choose to awaken, the wonder of all is within their reach. They need but to put out their hand and it shall be filled. Such a time of wonder and joy is ahead for all who truly seek and reach forth in love.

It is for those, such as you, to show and guide by gentleness, truth and sincerity of your way. They then shall see by example and witness by experience your truth and love, and thus have a desire to share in and share out this quality of their own self, with those about them. Step gently but in dignity of being and so, by example, guide without guiding.

Each of you has gifts and treasures to unfold, to be enjoyed and to be shared. Hold not tightly to the self, for in giving freely we receive that which we need and that which we desire. Desire not that which is another's, only that which may come freely and unencumbered and likewise, do not encumber another with your desires.

** *** **

Strangely, it is freedom of the self that we most fear, and, yet, it is this freedom that gives its all to the self and thence outward to all others. Know and trust the self that ye may know and trust all else.

Go now, in peace about your day.

Perception

Dear child of light, we are ever with you. Hold fast to this knowing. We walk with thee as one. So many walk this path with thee that it is almost impossible for you to perceive of the company in your day.

Times are changing but each shall face the change and walk with it in freedom and love. Those that have difficulty shall be guided forth in spirit and in flesh. For many take the step forward in their walk, so many travel that each shall be company for the other, not to support and hold, but to accompany and share, one with the other. This is not to say that they shall travel together upon this way, but in unison and harmony upon the way.

So much shall be achieved in each journey. The individual cannot as yet perceive their worth and the worth each shall bring to the journey, and indeed the journey to them. To accomplish but a few steps in wisdom is indeed a challenge that shall be well rewarded. We do not all need to travel a great distance, although some shall. For others, just a few steps will endow fellow travellers with the confidence and trust that they may require to continue *their* journey.

Upon your journey do not overload the self, but carry only that which you shall need, as indeed each traveller should lighten their load. How shall you learn upon the way if the back bends beneath a heavy load? Each must look ahead and about, that they may see and know the way, and thus to mark it for those who travel the same way.

*** *** ***

Although all roads lead to the One Source, it is known that many ways lead off or back, and so, to follow on a smooth way, we need guides and guide posts. Shall you and those who now seek and know, become these figures of signage? We ask that you shall. For we need co-operation and skill in which to place the pebbles at the feet of those who seek. Shall you co-operate? Then, skilfully and selflessly, place yourself as a pebble before the footfall of a traveller.

Know thee, that each pebble is counted. Each pebble is known. Do not be confused, rather do not analyse, for within it is known and the agreement made. We each have made our way to this moment in complete and trusting agreement. Now we move ahead in the knowing. Is it not a wonderful way, to be as one in our travels? Come, my child, we dance upon the way in joy and love.

There is so much to do in harmony and in truth. There are so many who wait to be about the business of love and light, and now we are in motion, so it shall flow forward as a great river of strength. Nothing shall bind the way of the movement, nothing shall divert the flow. Petals thrown upon the river shall flow to the source and be made whole again, as each comes to renewed life. Then, in turn, the renewal shall be shared with all who desire truth.

In this we progress together upon the way of truth and light, and the joy in the company of many souls, each aglow from within, as representative of the source in all. It is as if a cake has been mixed and is now ready to be baked, prior to the tasting and sharing.

** *** **

Go forth and enjoy in the partaking of thy fruits. Watch then as the many gather to share in the fruits of wisdom and love. In turn, they share their joy and so on, and so on; as it flows freely forth to all who but hold out a hand.

Know, child, that just the slightest movement of the hand is noted. The desire, the intent is known and thus acknowledged and acted upon. They need make but the slightest movement and we stand ready to transmit that which is required. Freely and in love of the all, we await the call

Now for this day, there is much about that requires attention. Go about thy needs, as we go about these and in unison all shall be accomplished.

Light

I awoke early with the thought to – 'Name this day, a day of light'.
[May 5th, 1998][i]

And so it shall be child. A day of light to be shared with as many as possible. The light flows outward from the One to each and every soul at all times, but there are times that it is known and indeed shown to the many. This is such a time – a day of days upon the earth plane.

In days to come there shall be talk of the light of this day, it shall be recorded as a light display within the universe, the energy of which shall touch many with its beauty. The universal rainbow, a sheath of colour so profound, it shall be noticed. It shall be recorded. For the few it shall be felt within as a pure burst of joy and of love, a love so gentle yet so deep, it too shall be recorded. You child shall feel its power – the power of the light within, reconnecting and refocusing.

There is no negativity that can break through the light, know you are surrounded in the protection and love of the light, as are those about you. We sometimes see life's experiences as negative but they are just experiences from which we grow and learn, moving ever outward and onward. We do not sit and wallow in the 'what if' or the 'maybe'. We get on and live our life and this is as it should be.[ii]

Responsibility Of Pleasure

To lead this life we must fairly balance responsibility and duty, with pleasure and creativity. Then in balance we are of profit to the self and to those who need our time and energy.

We do not, however, reduce or diminish their personal responsibilities by our care and attention. Again we support and assist others by example and with unconditional love. If we cannot share these, then we must step back or aside from the particular situation. Do not become dependent, nor allow another to become dependent upon you.

It is difficult to find a true balance but with practise and effort it is possible. Train the self, and others, to breathe deeply into the situation; be silent and reflect. Then being calm and rational, act, or not, as required. And remember always, the intent is known, the intent is powerful. Be aware, be guarded and truly know and recognise your intent at all times and in all situations.

Go, enjoy your day.

Rest

We are here, child, as ever, we walk with thee in all thy ways. Come let us walk away in harmony and joy. The still and gently glow of the day brings into focus the colours of nature.

Rest, child, all is well. Let the stillness of this day soak into your being. Days of rest must be treasured, for there is much work ahead and the rest days recharge the energies and the balance, both of which must be cherished.

My back door, open only a few inches and a Willy Wagtail came into view on my lawn. On closer inspection there are loads of birds – Honeyeaters, Doves and Silvereyes, in my garden at present. Thank you for touching my soul.

The Gift

A grand day and everything moves ahead, as it should. Each day brings one closer to the purpose and with new found courage, closer to the way of things, in all that we do and experience.

Such courage as you found today to make a choice, is that which we speak of. We understand the dilemma of being in human form, with the weight of responsibility that is placed upon each being. However, each must find a living balance as we have previously mentioned, with regard to responsibility and creativity.

That which you need shall be shown to you, for the gift has already been bestowed. Now you need but practice and learn the technique, and become familiar with the tools. This comes in good time, for you choose to move on ahead. Your teacher and constant companion is within and about you in all that you do. It is just that now you are in a transition period and everything is in readiness for you to take up the challenge.

Know that love in all, is your support and your guide. Work always with love at hand. For in love all is achievable and all is knowable.

Take heart, child, you are not alone on your journey, although at times it may seem so. We, and the many travel with you in all things.

This & That

It is a beautiful morning. We are here and would speak with thee, of this and that, and of so much more. To whom the information shall be given – as given unto all who may hear; and to thee when it shall be given – given as soon as may be possible and as needed.

Sadly, it is often only when they come in need that they ask and may listen, not realising that that which is about is available at all times. They but need to open only the mind and the heart to the One in all, and the All shall be made available, freely and without constraint.

Just as you sit in meditation, so should the many for it is this simple. It is we beings who complicate our own progress. Life in itself has become complicated and we along with it. It is in the silent stillness that we can again find ourselves, and in the finding we may then reconnect with the All and with the One in all.

There is no shame in taking our rest, for in rest the mind and body may again align with one another, and then in turn with the universal energy. Thus when truly rested and re-energised we may then put this universal energy to work for the *good of all*. Each one, as in the self, is of the all.

Be true to the self and in all else find the truth.

Healing

Greetings – breathe in the smoke of the sage essence and know its healing strength. Healing must take place in all aspects of life, not just in individual and isolated aspects. Do you know what we mean? *Yes.* All of mankind needs to have complete healing, and this may now be offered and yet, some may decline.

The healing process starts with the One and individuals now again look to the One. They then are soon joined by others and may stand strong in 'groups'. This does not mean they join or become members of groups, just that they know and recognise that they do not stand isolated and alone. Thus healing becomes a powerful energy that the many and indeed the whole, may share in and with, if so desired.

Healing may take place when we acknowledge the need for some change in one or other areas of our aspect. By this recognition of need for change we set forth the stone upon the pond and healing energy ripples outward thus, as a force unstoppable. As the individual ripples begin to entwine, so the energies become a powerful healing force for each and for the universe.

Then, in turn, others within the universal way may join with the process. Healing may be and is, such a gentle way in which to correct the imbalances. And yet, so many ignore or reject their own healing needs and processes. If they but realise the power and love they restrain, then indeed we should see wonders upon the earth plane.

Such wonders that have for so long now been neglected and thus have remained invisible. In truth and in love it is time now to step forward and to be made able, to once again see the way of things.

'Human beings' must again become truly human, and thus be about the business of speaking their truth and in that acting upon this truth. Much has been forgotten but the means now to remember is at hand. It is but for those who may choose to take up the recall, to act either by deed – put out your hand; or by intent – know in your mind, thinking only of the way. We may each speak our truth or walk our truth but in different ways and there are many different ways. However, it is the content and the intent of the deed that counts and in all, truth is the way to the One and to the healing of the all.

Healing may be found in a sound, a smell, a touch, a taste, a movement, a recognition but it is of no significance, if not acted upon, either for the self or for the Universal One who knows all. In helping the self we help others and thus reach out to the One in all, joining, once again, with the whole in reunion.

Gentle one, to thee I say – welcome home. We who are gathered rejoice in thy return. You have been about the world in your learning and now as a group we may be about the work. Your pen shall be busy but your hand shall not tire, and what shall fall forth upon the pages shall be of benefits to the many. In all you have learned well, although you do not often see that you have.

In the healing, words and images shall fall from your

mind as from a fountain. These shall be drunk, unto the very being of those who come forth to thee, as drops of healing elixir. They then shall share healing with those about them and the 'groups' and processes shall broaden upon the plains.

There is much to do and it shall be done, for we are about the way.

In all, child, go in light and love, and share forth thy truth.

Love Itself

'Time and tide' they say, wait for no man. Yet they may not be held back. Love, however, gives one the power to do just that. It is true love that conquers all. Divine love, the love that resides within *all* beings.

Too often we perceive love as an intense emotional state of being, we neglect the fact that we *are* love itself. Often when sharing ourselves and our love with others we give up the self to another, this is not true love. In turn they/we take this love and smother it to the self, this is not true love. True love is to hold open the hands and the heart.

So much more may be achieved by the offering of love unrestricted. However, this is a state of being that many of us must again, re-learn, for fear of not being loved makes many grasp and hold tightly to the slightest sign of love. Thus it is strangled, leaving emptiness and sadness, and the fear of turning to love again makes us turn our back on true joy, the joy of love unconditional and pure, in thought and deed.

It is the selfish possession of love, the holding fast to the self, that has distorted the intention of love. Love is a gift intended to be shared by all, gathered in, to be freely distributed outwardly. It is not a tool to be manipulated, nor to be used to manipulate another. It is and always will be a 'gift' of pure joy. It is not the gift that hurts the being, it is the way in which the gift is offered, that harm may occur.

** *** **

Too often it is held out, then suddenly snatched back, as the offeror still has hold of the gift. Fear prevents some, from holding out the hand open with the gift of love upon it. They fear the letting go. Try it, try letting go and you will be pleasantly and joyfully rewarded.

There are so many forms of love, the kiss of the sun upon the cheek, the drop of rain upon the hand. God offers love to each freely. Do not become embroiled in only a physical love, or, indeed, so much more love may pass thee by unseen, unknown and certainly unfelt.

Rejoice in the day and bring love and light to those about thee.

** *** **

Go now
and be about your day.
Share the words with those who would listen –
You and I together.

Acknowledgements

Blessings to family and friends, past and present, who have walked this path with me – patiently.

To the mediums Gwen and Marg who encouraged my development;

Catherine for her computer assistance and expertise;

Tracie for her spiritual and artistic guidance.

I am especially grateful to 'The Committee' for their continued love, guidance and wisdom, without their presence none of this would have been possible.

To all,
Thank you.

About the Author

Norma Fenttiman, an intuit of mind and senses was born in New South Wales. After the death of her father, Norma and her mother moved to Tasmania. There she met her future husband at age sixteen.

In 1970, with her husband and son, she settled in Western Australia.

Throughout these years she experienced numerous intuitive events, following in her mother's footsteps. Norma accepted these occurrences as being the normal way of things.

In her fifties she returned to university where a group of her friends persuaded her to acknowledge, and act upon, her intuitive abilities.

Desiring guidance, Norma began writing in diary form and the words began to fall upon the page.

Over a period of ten years these words and insights brought wonder and peace of mind as well as the belief and desire to share them with those about her.

---

[i] [May 8th 10.50pm(wst) Listening to a science program on the ABC radio – Jonathan Malley, is talking about a 'big bang' effect that was picked up on telescopes yesterday and is at present still being viewed/tracked. He said it occurred 500,000,000 light years ago and we are only now seeing it.]

www.ingramcontent.com/pod-product-compliance
Lightning Source LLC
Chambersburg PA
CBHW050316010526
44107CB00055B/2265